MICHAELA MORGAN

Illustrated by Guy Parker-Rees

OXFORD
UNIVERSITY PRESS

Great Clarendon Street, Oxford OX2 6DP

Oxford University Press is a department of the University of Oxford. It furthers the University's objective of excellence in research, scholarship, and education by publishing worldwide in

Oxford New York
Auckland Cape Town Dar es Salaam Hong Kong Karachi Kuala Lumpur Madrid Melbourne Mexico City Nairobi New Delhi Shanghai Taipei Toronto

With offices in
Argentina Austria Brazil Chile Czech Republic France Greece Guatemala Hungary Italy Japan Poland Portugal Singapore South Korea Switzerland Thailand Turkey Ukraine Vietnam

First published 1998
This edition 2005

British Library Cataloguing in Publication Data
Data available

ISBN 978-0-19-917968-8

9 10 8

Available in packs
Stage 10 More Stories A Pack of 6:
ISBN 978-0-19-917963-3
Stage 10 More Stories A Class Pack:
ISBN 978-0-19-917970-1
Guided Reading Cards also available:
ISBN 978-0-19-917972-5

Cover artwork by Guy Parker-Rees
Photograph of Michaela Morgan © Richard Drewe

Printed in China by Imago

Paper used in the production of this book is a natural, recyclable product made from wood grown in sustainable forests. The manufacturing process conforms to the environmental regulations of the country of origin.

1

Are you mad about
dinosaurs?
    Dexter is.
    Just look at his room.

At his birthday party Dexter had:

dinosaur balloons,

dinosaur cards,

dinosaur pizza,

and a
dinosaur cake.

Dexter and his friends played Pin the Horn on the Triceratops and Dexter won. It *was* his party after all.

But Dexter *didn't* have a real dinosaur. Even though he'd asked for one.

His Gran had given him a gerbil, but it wasn't the same.

Dexter had wished
and wished
and wished when he'd blown out his birthday cake candles.

He'd wished for any sort of dinosaur.

He'd opened his eyes and what had he seen?

Nine blown-out candles and a birthday cake.

His wish had not come true.

So, all in all, it was just as well that Dexter knew a wizard.

2

'What would you like for your birthday, this time?' asked the wizard.

'I'd like to go back in time, please,' said Dexter. 'I want to meet a dinosaur.'

'Back in time!' said the wizard. 'Oh dear me, no. It's much too dangerous back there.

You might be trodden on by
a tyrannosaurus.

Or bitten by a
brontosaurus.

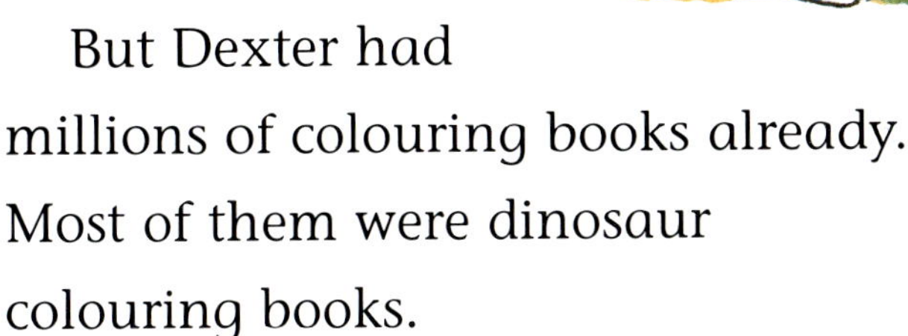

Or… sat on by
a stegosaurus.
Wouldn't you like
a nice colouring
book instead?'

But Dexter had millions of colouring books already. Most of them were dinosaur colouring books.

'Hmm… I suppose I could bring a dinosaur to *you,*' said the wizard. 'But I'd need to think up a spell. Let's see…'

Hocus pocus diplodocus,
Let's get a dinosaur!
A tyrannosaurus
Or a stegosaurus?
One or two? Or more?
Brontosaurus…gorgosaurus…
Anything would do.
A –

'Stop! STOP!' cried Dexter. 'Listen!'

'Aha!' cried the wizard. 'The dinosaur has landed.'

'Ah,' said the wizard, less happily. 'Another one.'

'Oops!' said the wizard. He was beginning to understand what was happening.

'Yes,' said Dexter. 'You've gone too far. You've got carried away. You've asked for too many!'

3

In the town there was panic. It was raining dinosaurs.

People were shaking and quaking, and running and hiding and SCREAMING.

'Don't worry,' Dexter said. 'Dinosaurs are mostly vegetarians.'

But even vegetarians can cause problems.

BIG problems.

The biggest problem of all was the meat-eating tyrannosaurus.

He (or she) was raging up and down the street. And his claws, jaws, and roars were all terrifying.

'Why, oh why did you have to ask for a tyrannosaurus rex?' moaned Dexter. 'Just look at it!'

4

The tyrannosaurus rex thundered down the High Street.

Its head was higher than a house.

Its eyes were bigger than your head.

And its teeth – oh, its teeth! They were sharper than razors and bigger than your boots.

'It seems to be looking for something,' muttered the wizard.

'It is,' wailed Dexter. 'It's looking for meat. Live meat. Run for it!'

Even the slowest dinosaurs knew it was time to move on – quickly. They ran through the town. They zoomed across zebra crossings. They trampled traffic lights.

Bang!

BANG!

BANNNNNNGGGGG!

The tyrannosaurus came down the High Street. It made the ground shake. It made the people shake too.

The tyrannosaurus looked over the tallest trees. It looked over the highest houses… but it did not look down at its own feet.

So it didn't notice the enormous hole in the ground. This hole had been made by the landing of a big fat brontosaurus.

It didn't see the hole.

It didn't step around the hole.

It just fell right into it.

Another sort of dinosaur could have climbed out.

But the tyrannosaurus couldn't.

It had fierce jaws.

It had sharp teeth.

But it had silly little arms.

So it couldn't pull itself out.

'Saved!' said Dexter. 'Now I can play with the friendly dinosaurs. That's what happens in all the dinosaur stories.'

Dexter wanted to play hide and seek with the dinosaurs.

He wanted to climb up their backs and slide down their necks. Just like in the books.

But the truth is, dinosaurs are not all that good at games. They are too stupid to understand the rules.

And they are too interested in eating to care about anything else.

'A dinosaur is not an ideal pet, you see,' said the wizard. 'You're better off with the gerbil after all.'

Dexter was beginning to think the wizard was right. And Dexter was beginning to worry. He tried to remember the wizard's spell. Was there a gorgosaurus in it?

A gorgosaurus is very like a tyrannosaurus. It is just as fierce. It is just as unfriendly. And Dexter could hear something crashing in the distance. It was getting closer.

5

CRASH! The sounds were getting nearer and nearer.

'All these dinosaurs have GOT to go home!' said Dexter. 'Now!'

Then he marched up to the nearest (and smallest) dinosaurs and flung his arms around them to hug them.

'You have to go now,' he said. 'Goodbye.'

Of course, they just went on eating, wallowing or standing around. Dexter was like a teeny tiny insect to them.

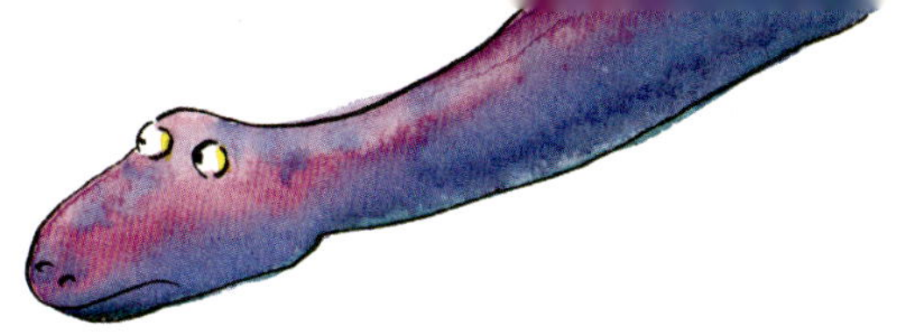

Bang! BANG! BANNNNNGGGGG!

The gorgosaurus was coming. This time there was no deep hole for it to fall into. And this time the wizard was having trouble with his spell.

Do you know how to undo a spell?

That's right, you just say it backwards. Easy! Or is it? Can you say all those dinosaurs' names backwards?

The wizard started off something like this:

It must have been more or less right because, one by one, dinosaurs started disappearing.

A very loud Paff! came from just outside the park. The gorgosaurus was gone!

Soon there wasn't a dinosaur left.

But there was a lot of mess. Dinosaurs are very messy creatures. And grown-ups don't like mess. Poor Dexter. It looked as if he was going to be in trouble!

But who can begin to understand grown-ups? What happens if you break one, little window?

They go completely mad.

Dexter's dinosaurs had broken hundreds of windows. Dexter's dinosaurs had knocked down walls. Dexter's dinosaurs had eaten the park.

When the grown-ups saw all this, what did they say to Dexter?

'Well done!' they said.

'The way you grabbed hold of those monsters and told them they had to go!' The grown-ups hugged Dexter. 'You've saved us!' they said.

So, all in all, everything ended happily, just as it should.

But the wizard couldn't help saying, 'I told you so. The best place for a dinosaur is in its own time – or in a book. You've learned a lesson, haven't you, Dexter. Dexter?'

But Dexter wasn't listening.

He was too busy thinking, 'What can I ask for next birthday?'

About the author

I wrote this story when my son was mad about dinosaurs. Some of the ideas in this story came from real life. For instance we had a dinosaur party with a dinosaur cake and we played Pin the Horn on the Triceratops. We never got a real dinosaur. That bit is made up. A lot of my stories start in real life and then they grow when I start to wonder 'What would happen if...?'